Jogging Through Space

Sixty Pathways to Feeling Better

Mary Morgan McKnight

© Copyright 2002 Mary Morgan McKnight. All rights reserved.
No part of this publication may be reproduced, stored in a retrieval system, or transmitted, in any form or by any means, electronic, mechanical, photocopying, recording, or otherwise, without the written prior permission of the author.
Printed in Victoria, Canada

National Library of Canada Cataloguing in Publication

McKnight, Mary Morgan, 1945-
Jogging through space / Mary Morgan McKnight.
ISBN 1-55369-669-7
1. McKnight, Mary Morgan, 1945- --Health. 2. Brain--Surgery--Patients--Biography. I. Title.
RD594.M33 2002   362.1'97481'0092   C2002-902913-9

This book was published *on-demand* **in cooperation with Trafford Publishing.**
On-demand publishing is a unique process and service of making a book available for retail sale to the public taking advantage of on-demand manufacturing and Internet marketing. **On-demand publishing** includes promotions, retail sales, manufacturing, order fulfilment, accounting and collecting royalties on behalf of the author.

TRAFFORD

Suite 6E, 2333 Government St., Victoria, B.C. V8T 4P4, CANADA
Phone   250-383-6864   Toll-free   1-888-232-4444 (Canada & US)
Fax   250-383-6804   E-mail   sales@trafford.com
Web site www.trafford.com   TRAFFORD PUBLISHING IS A DIVISION OF TRAFFORD HOLDINGS LTD.
Trafford Catalogue #02-0482   www.trafford.com/robots/02-0482.html

10   9   8   7   6   5   4   3   2

Dedicated

to

the readers of this book.

If anyone feels better as a

result of reading any part

of *Jogging Through Space,*

then its purpose has been

accomplished!

Appreciation to...
David, my husband and friend, who edited this
material and put his magic to my words;

And to my friends...
Roger Conant, who graciously offered
to type this manuscript;

Katie Letcher Lyle, for her unfailing encouragement
and help toward publication;

Patricia Wells, for editing advice and for
making corrections on the manuscript;

Wendy Bush Hackney, for all the graphic design work.

About the Author

Mary Morgan McKnight has a Bachelor of Arts degree in Psychology and English from McMaster University in Hamilton, Ontario, Canada, and a Master of Divinity degree from McMaster Divinity College.

Mary has worked as a teacher, pastoral minister, and spiritual director of a Quaker Retreat Center. She is creator of *Calm Cards*, the *Pocket Problem-Solver*, and an adult-children's book, *The Gift Agreement* (1988), offering a solution to war. She has authored two books of poetry, *A Voice of the Heart* (1992), and *Outside In* (1996), and co-written a musical, *Mamahuhu*, which opened in London in 1992. In 1999 she wrote *Aunt Mary's Woodstove Cookbook*.

Mary is currently writing and researching alternate healing techniques.

A Canadian, she lives in Virginia with her teacher-husband, David.

Contents

	Dedication	iii
	Appreciation	iv
	About the Author	v
	Table of Contents	vi
	Introduction	1
	About the Pathways	3
	Stories & Pathways	
1.	Dream Elevator	6
2.	Dark to Light	8
3.	Multiple Sclerosis	12
4.	Scans and Grams	16
5.	A Vision of Strength	20
6.	Memory Bank	22
7.	A Powerful Gift	24
8.	Making a Will	26
9.	Operation Day	28
10.	Near-Death Experience	30
11.	Turn to the Light	34
12.	Please— No Lights!	36
13.	Spit	38
14.	Ninety-three Years Old	40
15.	A Child Angel	42
16.	Hospital Psychosis	46
17.	Laughter	50
18.	Watermelon	52
19.	Jogging Through Space	54
20.	Self Massage	56
21.	Pink & Yellow Tulips	60
22.	Wash	62
23.	Music	64
24.	Elysha	66
25.	Seeing Eye Dog	70
26.	Lady in a Blue Dress	72
27.	Seasons	76
28.	A Scream in the Night	78
29.	Speech Therapy	80
30.	Awesome Beauty	82
31.	Savoring the Taste	84

32. Housewalking	86	
33. Acute Pain	88	
34. Sick Days	90	
35. Downslide	94	
36. Forgiveness Letters	98	
37. A Crystal House	100	
38. Slow Flow	102	
39. Rainbow Man	104	
40. Pendle Hill	108	
41. Follow Your Passion	112	
42. Lawn Mowing	116	
43. Calm Cards	120	
44. Firbank Field	122	
45. Journaling	124	
46. Friends	128	
47. A Healing Cabin	130	
48. Hypnosis	134	
49. Quaker Meeting	136	
50. The Blue Liquid	142	
51. Making Lists	144	
52. Hands-on Help	146	
53. Sadsbury Silence	150	
54. Creative Choices	154	
55. The Umbrella Plant	156	
56. Claim Divine Power	158	
57. Dream Detective	160	
58. Epilogue	162	
59. David	164	
60. Postscript	166	

Appendix

1. Self-Massage	174
2. Anatomy Breathing	177
3. Slow Flow	180
Bedexercises I	181
Bedexercises II	184
Copy Cats	187
4. Dream Detective	192

Introduction

At 37 years of age and involved in an active church ministry, I underwent surgery to have a brain tumor removed. The surgeon said I would have died within a month if the tumor had not been taken out immediately. I am very thankful that his action saved my life, and grateful to the many people who have helped me in my recovery.

Recovering has been a long road. I had to learn to eat, walk, and talk all over again. Other side-effects of the surgery have been, at times, quite horrendous — including severe seizures, blinding head pain and all-day vomiting. There were days that I wished I had died.

Through it all I have been searching for ways to help myself — to regain health. I gradually discovered things to do that made me feel better. When something worked especially well, I would use it often. In this book I offer my story, some of it taken directly from journal entries written at the time. I have included suggestions that helped *me* feel better in various situations. My hope is that there will be something here that will help *you*.

There are 60 Pathways suggested in this book. They may lead you into *other* pathways. However, they are *not substitutes* for traditional medical care. Sometimes pain's greatest gift to us is to tell us that something happening in our body needs medical attention.

About the Pathways

*Try the simple suggestions
presented in this book, if you like,
observing their effects
and incorporating what works for you
into a "feel-better program."
And don't work too hard
or strain at feeling better.
Strain is tension-producing in itself!
Just relax and listen to my story —
learning some feel-better ideas
as you go along.*

Stories & Pathways

1 Dream Elevator

 On May 29th, 1981 I wrote in my journal:

Today I worked on my radio show, then visited with several parishioners, and finally did some worship preparation. I feel tired because I've been awake too many hours and working hard. There is a lot of responsibility involved in being an effective helper. Sometimes I feel like the old woman who lived in a shoe, and had so many children, she didn't know what to do!

In the night I awoke from a dream in which I was in a highrise elevator that moved as fast as a turbo train. The elevator was crowded, and when it stopped at my floor I wanted to get out! Before I woke up a voice in the dream seemed to shout: "This will affect you within an inch of your life!"

The dream seemed to be saying: *Slow down!* ∎

Pathway 1

*To help you slow down,
write yourself into
your datebook!
Make relaxation
appointments
with yourself
and others.*

2
Dark to Light

 On June 12th, 1981 I wrote in my journal:

I have felt pressure in my head and neck all day. It feels so strange— like it's running through my jaws and teeth and nose and glands. This morning I went to clean my teeth, and they felt like they had "moved." I washed my face, but it didn't feel like my face. This doesn't make the least bit of sense, and I don't want to push any panic buttons. Maybe it's just the tail-end of a cold I have had, or the result of working too hard and being under a lot of pressure.

Suddenly I was feeling tears of frustration over whatever was wrong. The

2

tears were hardly in my eyes when I realized it was raining outside. I walked to my window to look out. A soft spring-like rain was falling, and the setting sun was shining brilliantly through dark clouds. The sunlight was reflecting red and gold on an old church steeple in town, and as I watched the steeple a rainbow appeared.

Oh, how much beyond words! It was a double rainbow right over the steeple! For the next twenty minutes I lived in the world of the sky. I pulled my boots on and walked out on my balcony to get the full feel of it. The sunset was glorious: purple, orange, and rose, darks and lights. And the rainbow

2

lasted well after sunset. I don't understand this. The refraction must have been bouncing off the clouds.

For me it was all a sign of hope. I don't know what the strange sensations in my face mean. But I feel hopeful that whatever happens, it's going to be all right. ∎

Pathway 2

*When the
clouds of life
are at their darkest,
look for
some sign of hope—
something
to be
thankful for!*

3
Multiple Sclerosis

I phoned the neurologist I had seen about a ringing sound in my ears. In his office, he looked into my eyes with a light. "The left eye is puffy where the optic nerve comes in," he said. "It's called 'optic neuritis'." He hopes that a drug he has prescribed can control this. "It might spread to the other eye. And there's a 25 percent chance the condition may show up in other places— in which case it's called 'multiple sclerosis'."

Multiple sclerosis! When he said this to me, the doctor was speaking quietly from behind his desk. I was still sitting in the red chair I had taken upon entering his office. But everything, literally everything, changed with the sound of those words. They went merry-go-rounding in my mind: "multiple ... multiple ... multiply up."

The doctor handed me a prescription, and asked me to come back in a month. A month seemed like

3

such a long time! Then I was walking toward the receptionist's desk. Was it me walking— or a mechanical toy? I felt like a broken doll. But I would be a brave one....

I turned toward the waiting room and smiled thankfully at my friend, Jay, who was rising from his chair like a tall, strong patch of sunshine.

Jay had spent the previous month in Europe on a singing tour. But here he was back from Paris, and opening the waiting room door for us to go out into a sunny day.

I told him slowly what the doctor had said, and asked if he would drive me to a pharmacy for a prescription. I next explained some of the examining procedures I had gone through.

His hand reached over to grab mine. We were by this time driving in traffic. I hesitated before I finished

3

telling him what the neurologist had said to me: "And there's a 25 percent chance that this could show up in other places... in which case it is called 'multiple sclerosis'."

Jay's hand was gripping mine like steel, and my eyes were raining tears... tears of fears, and tears of relief in telling it out.

There was a long pause.

"Let's concentrate on the 75 percent chance that it's not multiple sclerosis," he said finally. "And if it turns out otherwise, we'll face that when we know it."

"75 percent hopeful sounds better than 25, doesn't it?" I pushed the words out as I dried my tears. But I felt unconvinced.

Jay parked the car by the pharmacy, and we went in for the prescription. ■

Pathway 3

*Journal about
your deepest thoughts and feelings
in a notebook,
or talk with someone who will listen
with caring and without judgement.
Write, talk, or act out ideas and feelings.
It's okay to feel your feelings.
It sometimes helps to laugh,
cry or punch a pillow.
Set a time limit on negative expression,
but get it out—
and feel better!*

4
Scans & Grams

I sought a second opinion from a neurologist my father recommended. After seeing me, he booked a CT scan which revealed a brain tumor. "It will have to come out or it could cause nerve and brain damage," he said.

This was confirmed by a neurosurgeon. And before I knew what was happening, I was in a hospital undergoing tests.

Of the tests, the angiogram was the worst, not because it was overly complicated or very invasive, but

4

because the way I was told about it filled me with fear.

The technician informed me that I could become paralyzed, or go blind, as a result of the procedure. He said that there was very little chance of either of these things happening; but it did happen sometimes and they were obligated to tell me before I gave permission for the test, because of a possible liability suit!

"I won't have the test, then," I said. The neurosurgeon felt that it was important for me to have this test before

4

undergoing surgery because of the valuable information it would give him about the location, size, and form of the tumor.

I was frightened and confused. What the doctor said seemed to make sense. I signed the papers to waive liability for the angiogram. ∎

Pathway 4

*Don't allow
anyone to bulldoze you
into doing something
without considering your options,
weighing pros and cons,
and making the best decision you can.
Repressing
your own thoughts and feelings
is not a "feel-better" response!*

5
A Vision of Strength

At the time of the angiogram I was wheeled on a stretcher to a testing room full of strange machinery. I was scared. I looked at the machinery and wondered if it might be the last thing I would ever see.

The technicians started the machine and a doctor came in to do the test. It was so noisy that I felt as if I was in a storm. The word "storm" seemed to be a word for me to hang onto. I closed my eyes and remembered Jesus being in a storm. His disciples were frightened. Suddenly I had a clear picture of Jesus standing up in my "boat," and saying, "Why are you afraid? Where is your faith?" I immediately felt completely calm.

The test went quickly and easily. The doctor held up two fingers in front of my eyes. "How many fingers am I holding up?" he asked. "Two," I replied. He asked me to move my fingers and toes. I did this effortlessly. ■

Pathway 5

*There were times
when I didn't feel strong enough
to pull together any resources.
I felt tired, scared and confused.
I had just enough strength
to give the entire situation over
to a higher Spiritual power—
to be open to help
from another source
and rest in that.*

6 Memory Bank

If anyone but Jesus had asked me, "Why are you afraid? Where is your faith?" I probably would have felt offended. But these words were just what I needed to calm me down at the moment I heard them.

Words are powerful! When I was a child, I listened to uplifting stories, and memorized verses, poems, and other "affirmations" that stayed with me. In later years I was able to draw on such verses and affirmations to give me strength, comfort and a sense of peace in times of difficulty. One of the verses that helps me the most is these words of Jesus:

Peace I leave with you, my peace I give unto you. Not as the world gives, give I unto you. Let not your heart be troubled. Neither let it be afraid.

An affirmation I like is: *All is well. I am loved.*

Or sometimes I simply repeat a word that has been soothing to me, like: *Calm.* ■

Pathway 6

*Go into your memory bank
and pick out a few uplifting,
affirming, peace-giving sayings or words.
Even memorize some new ones.
Include some affirmations of yourself!
You can then draw upon them
for strength and peace
when you need them.*

7
A Powerful Gift

The medical tests went on for about a week. During that time I seemed to deteriorate. I was losing balance, hearing and speech as the growing tumor pressed on nerves in my brain.

On the night before my surgery to remove the tumor, a nurse on the hospital ward came into my room with a gift for me. It was a crucifix. When I cradled it in my arms it had a powerful effect on me. I started to cry... so much humility, love, and pain in the form of Christ on the cross. It comforted me to identify with this suffering Jesus. ■

Pathway 7

*Hold in your hand
an object
which has
meaningful associations
for you –
a picture ... a sacred object ...
something from nature ...
a stuffed animal!*

8 Making A Will

It occured to me that this was a serious operation I was about to undergo! I hastily wrote out a will, and gave it to my brother when he came to see me before the surgery. If I was going to pass out of this life, I wanted certain people to have particular cherished possessions.

When I handed him the will, tears formed in my brother's eyes. He smiled and said, "I'll give this paper back to you in a few days."

Pathway 8

*It is a feel-better thing
to bring order into your life.
Finish up unfinished business!
There is a sense of satisfaction
in doing this.
The hardest part
is the first few minutes
of working on it.*

9 Operation Day

On the morning of the operation, I remember crying when I said goodbye to my parents at the operating room door. Suddenly the whole thing seemed so final.

The surgery lasted eleven hours. When I woke up I was in the Intensive Care Unit of the hospital. There were strange machines around me and attached to me. I felt as if the left side of my nose had collapsed, and that I needed to concentrate on every breath. It was such an effort, and I was afraid when I couldn't breathe.

The thought went through my mind: "You're going to die— and you haven't really lived!" I had been racing through my life: earning a living, trying to minister to everyone else's needs, trying to do everything "perfectly."

But I hadn't really appreciated life enough— people, nature, myself. I hadn't stopped to smell the roses! I thought, "If I had it to do over again, I would live my life differently." ■

Pathway 9

"Stop to smell the roses"
and
feel better!

10
Near Death Experience

I had a fleeting sensation that my head flopped to one side, although I hadn't moved it. I felt myself "rising" through my shoulders. It was like take-off in an airplane. I heard a far-off alarm bell sounding. And then I seemed to be surrounded by the most beautiful music I have ever heard. There were no musical instruments— just thousands and thousands of voices singing in harmony. I wanted to write the music down, but then realized I couldn't do that because I was floating near the ceiling of the Intensive Care Unit! So I just floated and listened.

It seemed as though I had a heightened awareness of everything that was happening in the Intensive Care Unit. I thought I heard people's conversations, and felt their pain.

10

I saw a group of medical staff gathered around a bed near mine. I sensed that the patient on the bed was having a heart attack, and I thought, "I wish I could help him." At that moment a rainbow appeared to reach from the ceiling down to the man— and he sat up!

Then I was in a misty place. It was like a field of foggy light, and as I looked toward it I saw my grandfather. He came to me and hugged me. He laughed, and said, "I am ninety-three years old now." This seemed to be some kind of a joke to him. (My grandfather had died when he was seventy.)

Then I saw a radiant light in the distance. I just wanted to go toward it. It seemed to shine with all the love and warmth associated with home, best friends and loved ones.

10

Behind me I heard a deep bass voice which seemed to split everything. It said, "God is not so much a trinity as a magnanimity. God is in everything." The voice broke into laughter and said, "Life is a joke!"

I continued to move toward the light at a great speed. Then suddenly I was stopped by a gate-like place. I sensed that I was being given a choice either to go on, or to return to my body. It felt so light and free to be out of a heavy, painful body.

However, I sensed that many people were praying for me—my family and friends. I wanted to live so that I could be with them again, share whatever I was experiencing in the out-of-body episode, and appreciate life more authentically. ■

Pathway 10

*I feel better
when I can tell a story
from my life experience
to someone who will listen
with interest
and without judgment.
Then I like to hear
a story of theirs in return.
Tell somebody
one of your stories!*

11
Turn to the Light

Just as I thought about wanting to live, I was back in my body. I felt the bars of my hospital bed, and the warmth of sunlight shining through the window of the Intensive Care Unit. It was splashing all over my bed.

I remembered some words which a woman had shared with me a few weeks earlier: "If you can't do anything else, just turn toward the light. A slow, gentle turning— that is all." ∎

Pathway 11

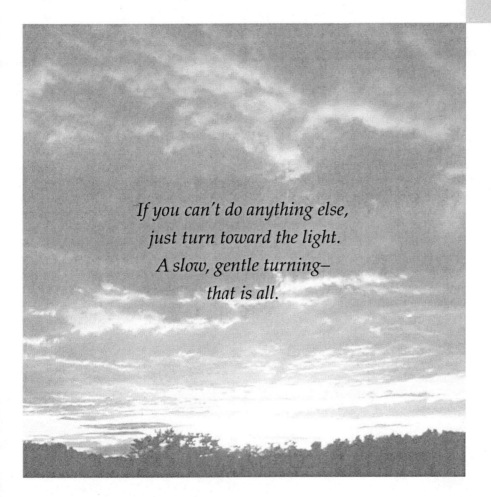

*If you can't do anything else,
just turn toward the light.
A slow, gentle turning—
that is all.*

12
Please— No Lights!

I lost consciousness, and when I woke up again light was blazing into my eyes from an overhead fluorescent lamp. The light was stark, sharp and painful. Commotion hit my consciousness with a bustling intensity.

I tried to speak, to protest— but I couldn't form any words. My face felt strange, and my throat wouldn't move.

I frantically grabbed at the coat-sleeve of a doctor by my bed. His face danced crazily in front of my eyes. I reached for the pen clipped in his coat pocket, and he smiled in surprise and handed me a paper to write on.

With great effort I printed these words:

"Please— no lights. They hurt my eyes." ■

Pathway 12

Ask on your own behalf!
Put your longings
on the line.
Ask people for help.
Pray for angels to guide you.
Good communication
helps.

13
Spit

I slipped in and out of consciousness, more out than in. The next time I became aware of my surroundings I heard the "tick, tick" sounds of machines near to my bed. The blazing lights had gone, and I saw that I was lying in a small glass cubicle away from lights, noise and commotion.

My mouth was drooling, and there was a small puddle of spit on my pillow. My eyes focused on the puddle. And the thought went through my mind, "This spit is very important!" Another part of me said that such an idea was crazy. Yet the thought seemed to be a great revelation to me about life and health! ■

Pathway 13

*Spit
has natural healing qualities.
Jesus used it
to restore hearing and sight.
I have read
that saliva is a good thing to apply to a cut.
Some of the most healing substances
are naturally-occurring.*

14
Ninety-three Years Old

My father came in to see me and I tried to tell him, by writing it down, about the near-death experience I had had. I thought he might wonder if I had gone crazy. But he listened to me with great interest. I wrote, "And I saw Grandpa. He said he was ninety-three years old now." My father quietly did some figuring on a paper and then said, "By golly, your grandfather would be ninety-three years old now if he had lived!"

It helped that my father didn't judge me, but truly listened to what I had to say.

The care that I received from my parents during my illness was very important in my recovery! ■

Pathway 14

*Take a moment
to feel care for a person,
an animal,
any living thing.
Nurture, and
be nurtured.*

15
A Child Angel

That night, after I had closed my eyes and before I went to sleep, I had a vision of a child angel dressed in shining light clothes. He reached toward me and said, "I want you to be still and hold the light." I felt my hands tingle, and it seemed like they were dancing with light, with all the colors of the rainbow and more. The colors seemed to move around me and through me. The angel said, "Everything is going to be all right!"

Perhaps this was a dream; yet I felt that I was awake. Possibly it was a vision or

15

apparition or hallucination. Whatever it was, it comforted me, encouraged me, and filled me with joy.

Since my near-death experience I have had other visions of another reality. A person from another world may suddenly appear, just standing quietly— or even pass by without looking at me. My reaction to these experiences is one of surprise and curiosity. Who are these people? What are they doing? I see them clearly, and then they are gone. Has my near-death experience opened a visual

15

channel to another dimension? It is something I seem to have no control over. Nor do most of the people have meaning to me.

But the child angel had tremendous meaning. At the moment he spoke to me, I knew that whether I lived or died, everything was going to be all right! A weight of uncertainty and fear left me. ∎

Pathway 15

*Recall
the message of many angels
reported in literature:
"Fear not!
Everything
is going to be all right!"*

16
Hospital Psychosis

Before my surgery a nurse friend of mine had offered to be a "special nurse" for me at any time that I needed extra care following surgery. I discovered later that she was told that I was too sick to have anyone take care of me except the I.C.U. nurses.

Time crawled. It seemed interminable! I felt feverish, and often my head ached intolerably. During one of these periods of discomfort, I glanced at a sink in the corner of my cubicle. Water was dripping slowly from the faucet, and I wished very

16

much to have a cold washcloth on my forehead. But there was no way for me to extricate myself from the machines around me and the sidebars on my bed. I pushed a buzzer to summon a nurse. When one appeared, I tried to form the words "cold water, wash cloth." She misunderstood me and brought a glass of water. She held it to my lips, not realizing that my throat was paralyzed and I couldn't swallow. My attempts to swallow a liquid had caused severe choking spells which cut off my air. Realizing that there was a towel beside my

16

pillow, with my free hand I knocked the glass of water she was holding so that it would spill on the towel. Then I lifted the towel to my aching forehead. I saw from the expression on the nurse's face that I had offended her. But I simply didn't know how else to communicate with her.

That was the beginning of a series of events which, taken together, made me believe, in my drugged state, that some members of the nursing staff were trying to kill me! Possibly this is what is meant by "hospital psychosis." ■

Pathway 16

*It is not uncommon to hear about a relative or
acquaintance who has undergone a personality change—
"flipped out!"—while in the hospital,
or even confined to a sick bed at home.
Friends and hospital staff often distance themselves from these
patients because of the unpleasantness
of such situations, or their own hurt feelings.
At the root of the anger, despair or uncharacteristic behavior of
the sick person may be a mixture of
medication, sensory deprivation, and a basic fear
that they have lost control of their lives.*
Please try to understand this!
*Attempt to give the sick person as much control
over their own life as they can comfortably handle. Your
understanding and love in the face
of such strange behavior can be a key
in helping the person feel better!*

17
Laughter

One day I opened my eyes and my brother, Franklin, was standing by my bed holding a mop! My surprise about the mop must have been communicated by the expression on my face!

He laughed, kissed me on the forehead, and told me that he thought he might have a problem getting in to see me since my visitor's list was so restricted. So he wore institutional-looking clothes— and even got a mop!

A smile started to form on my face. Smiling seemed strange because my face was paralyzed on the left side due to cut nerves. But I was certainly smiling inside, seeing him standing there with a mop.

Franklin knew that I couldn't talk. There was no chair in the I.C.U. for him to sit on so he leaned against the bedrail, took my hand, and quietly talked to me about things that had happened to him since I had last seen him. Many of these stories were humorous— and humor is a great feel-better therapy! ∎

Pathway 17

*Laughter acts
as an internal "massage,"
and affects body chemistry
in a positive way.
Seek people or situations
that make you laugh.
Read the comics,
or jokes from books or the Internet.
Or watch a funny T.V. program
or video!*

18
Watermelon

By writing I communicated to my brother that I had a longing to eat some watermelon. Somehow it seemed to me that I might be able to swallow it.

Franklin disappeared for several hours and when he came back he had a small jar containing some watermelon that had been pureed in a blender.

He explained to me that he had bought the watermelon, "broken into" our parents' house to use their blender (they were not home at the time), seeded the fruit and pureed it.

He had a spoon with him and commenced to put a small amount of the watery pink slush into my mouth. It tasted sweet and refreshing on my tongue. I swallowed— and when I realized that it had gone down my throat, I started to cry. Tears of relief and joy that I could finally swallow something! After that I progressed to liquids, soups, and baby food. This was a major turning-point in my return to health. ∎

Pathway 18

*Everyone
feels better
when they receive
loving attention.
It can be
life-changing!*

19
Jogging Through Space

One night when I was lying in my hospital bed, still unable to walk, I had a dream. I was jogging through space—through clear blue sky and white clouds. I jogged through the air, and bounced on the clouds. My body felt light, physically strong, and free from pain. It was on the following morning that I took my first steps. Somehow I connect learning to walk again with that dream.*

It could be that my "dream self" was telling me that my body was ready to walk again. Possibly there was a positive change in my body chemistry, or mental attitude, that began with that nighttime jog. ∎

For a dream interpretation process, see page 192.

Pathway 19

*Pay attention to your dreams!
Write down key words
about the dream
that will bring it back to mind
if you should decide to try to interpret it.
I sometimes write on a piece of paper
before going to bed,
asking for a dream of guidance, or of well-being.
The act of writing down this request
focuses the unconscious mind on
providing what you ask for.*

20 Self Massage

My parents' minister, Rev. Elmer Anderson, was one of the few visitors who was allowed in to see me. He not only strengthened me with his prayers, but asked me a question that few people asked: "What would you like me to do for you?" After a long pause to think, I pointed to the drawer where my cosmetic bag was, and managed to convey to him that I would like him to take the lotion out and rub my neck and back. This he did. And every time he came to visit, he blessed me with a mixture of prayers, talk— and a neck-and-back rub.

20

Later on, the importance of those massages inspired me to work out a self-massage routine. One obvious advantage of a self-massage is that you can do it whenever you feel like it. Also, massaging yourself gives that period of time meaning and purpose. A great frustration for me was not feeling very useful to myself or anyone else when I had to lie in bed all day, day after day. Doing self-massage gave me back a sense of personal control of my life.

Another advantage of self-massage is being able to apply just the right amount

20

of hand-pressure to different parts of your body. If there is a place that doesn't feel good to touch, or to touch too firmly, you can adjust the pressure.

My self-massage routine is described step-by-step in the Appendix (page 174), if you wish to try the system I have developed through the years. Of course you can develop your own system of massaging your body, experimenting creatively. ∎

Pathway 20

*Ask someone you care about
to rub your back.
Relax and enjoy it.
Or move your own hands
over any area of your body
which feels tense.*

21 Pink & Yellow Tulips

On the day that I was released from the Intensive Care Unit to go to a regular hospital ward, my friend, Jay, came and accompanied me on my move. When my stretcher entered the new hospital room, I felt like I was entering a garden. Jay had brought in a half dozen flower pots filled with pink and yellow tulips. What a wonderful sight they were! ■

Pathway 21

*Your physical environment can make a difference
in how stressed— or well— you feel.
Quiet colors, familiar surroundings and beauty,
such as flowers,
can change body chemistry and
contribute
to a feel-better state.*

22
Wash

The nurses on Ward 44 where I now resided were wonderful to me. Of course, I was feeling better, and I'm sure that made a difference in my perception of what I was experiencing. Within a few hours of my arrival in the new ward my IV tube was taken out, and I was wheeled to a tub room for a bath— my first one in two weeks.

I felt like a child at play as I soaped down and splashed the water all over me. It was definitely a feel-better experience! ∎

Pathway 22

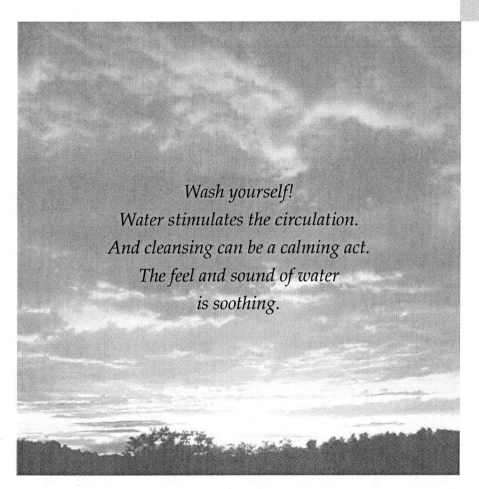

Wash yourself!
Water stimulates the circulation.
And cleansing can be a calming act.
The feel and sound of water
is soothing.

23
Music

A friend came to visit and brought me a cassette player and some tapes. I hungered to listen to music, and was very grateful for the gift. One day I slipped a music cassette into the player, turned the volume where it was audible to me, and began to listen. ∎

Pathway 23

Listen to music!
Something pleasing to you.
Modern researchers have demonstrated that the brain
needs 3 billion stimuli per second
for at least 4 1/2 hours a day in order
for a person to be wide awake!
Much of this stimuli comes through the ear,
which is a key charging mechanism of the brain.
Music can create harmony,
bring you back toward balance, straighten posture,
express feelings, and
be a connection with other people or
a meaningful time.

24
Elysha

On the day I began to listen to music, I was just beginning to enjoy the sounds and rhythm when a young man burst into my room yelling, "Turn it down! Turn it down!"

I must have looked a sight— with part of my head shaved, bandages, and my face collapsed on the left side — for when he saw me and realized my condition, he began to apologize profusely for bursting in on me. I turned the sound down; and then he

24

explained that his wife, Elysha, who was across the hall from me, had also had brain surgery, and couldn't stand the noise. He was in tears.

I haltingly formed a few words of apology for having the sound so loud. During the surgery my hearing nerve had been cut in removing the brain tumor which had attached to that nerve. Now I was deaf in one ear, and was beginning to realize what it meant to have diminished hearing.

24

The young man insisted that I listen to my music, and said it was encouraging to him to see me doing so well. Maybe Elysha would get better, too.

That began a relationship between me and Elysha's family. They were always so encouraged by my progress, and I reached out to them, identifying with Elysha and what she was going through. ∎

Pathway 24

*Draw inspiration
from others
who are doing well.
Ask what is helping them
to feel better!*

25 Seeing Eye Dog

I loved to go to the physiotherapy department. It was a room with pulleys, weights, benches and bars. But what I loved most about it was that when I was wheeled to "physio," I was greeted by a beautiful Golden Retriever dog! The physiotherapist was blind, and his dog not only assisted him, but the patients as well. The dog would allow me to hug him. And he seemed to know when I was progressing in my walking practice, and barked approval.

My main physiotherapy task was to practice walking between two waist-high bars, at first holding onto the bars, and then gradually walking without them. It was easier to take a step when I concentrated hard on the floor. If I looked up, I would lose my balance and pitch to one side.

The doctor explained that my body would gradually compensate for the nerve being cut that fed my inner ear balancing mechanism. I have since learned to balance with my eyes! ■

Pathway 25

*Today
Hug yourself...
Hug a friend...
Hug an animal...
Hug a tree!
Hugging
is an exchange of life-energy
and can help you feel better!*

26 Lady in a Blue Dress

One day I practiced walking in the hall of Ward 44. There was a silver handrail running the length of the hall for patients to hold onto if needed. I concentrated on one step at a time. That's all I had to do: one step at a time.

As I came to the second doorway along the hall, I saw a tall, thin lady in a blue dress standing in the room. She was leaning against a wall and crying. I was aware of perceiving feelings that were not my own. I felt like I was crying... and waiting... waiting for a husband who was

26

in the operating room undergoing surgery. I had no husband who was being operated on! But I felt like I did, and I was experiencing so much anguish about the whole situation that it almost knocked me over. I looked into the woman's eyes, and she blinked back at me through her tears. Then my eyes filled with tears, and her mood began to change. As her tears stopped she came out into the hallway, where I was still hanging onto the wall railing.

"It's all right," she said.

26

"Yes," I nodded, "it's all right." I felt like I had helped her by my total identification with her.

Still today when I am with people I sometimes sense their feelings and "know" things whether I want to or not. My way of handling this has been to block out any unwanted feelings, and focus on the love that is at the heart of each person. ■

Pathway 26

What you focus on, you energize!
Focus on others with love.
It will energize them,
and trigger
deep positive forces.

27
Seasons

I walked slowly back to my room, feeling both elated and exhausted. Elated because I thought I had helped the woman in the blue dress, and exhausted because I didn't quite have enough energy to be experiencing someone else's intense feelings as if they were my own.

When I got back to my hospital room I felt drained of energy, dizzy, nauseous, feverish— and I was experiencing a high-pitched whining sound in my head. I had a desperate desire to be away from people. I felt like I needed to take care of me, to rest and be quiet. ∎

Pathway 27

*"To everything
there is a season,
and a time
for every purpose
under heaven."*
There is a time
to rest
and be quiet.

28
A Scream in the Night

One night I woke up to the sound of slamming doors. People were yelling. It sounded high-pitched and hysterical. I lay in bed feeling something of deep tragedy in someone's life. There was a blood-curdling scream, and I wondered if someone had just lost a loved one. I said a prayer for those involved, and immediately felt a warm, pulsing presence. I sensed that I was feeling another person's soul. It seemed "kooky," and I couldn't explain it. But the feeling was there, and my love went out to someone or something I knew nothing about. ∎

Pathway 28

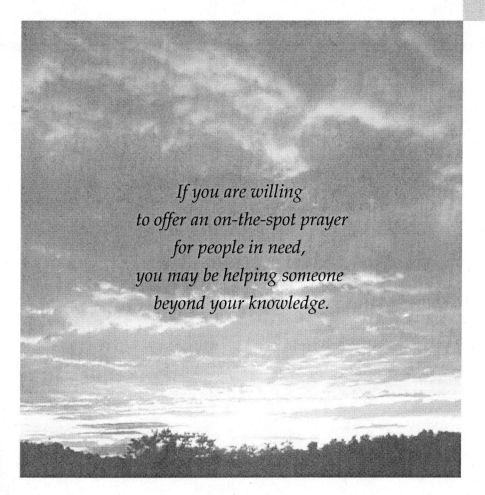

*If you are willing
to offer an on-the-spot prayer
for people in need,
you may be helping someone
beyond your knowledge.*

29 Speech Therapy

A speech therapist came to help me with forming words and sentences. I began to practice exercises she gave me to do— like uttering a vowel sound with sliding notes, and trying to say the sentence, "Now is the hour for all good folks to come to the aid of the party."

It began to help. With practice, I could do an octave of notes. I began to speak again, although every time I opened my mouth my face felt strange, and my throat would sometimes catch in painful muscle spasms.

Singing was another matter. It took tremendous effort to mouth the words of a song. Trying to sing felt to my face like running up a steep hill would feel to an out-of-condition runner.

The key seemed to be to be grateful for what voice I had, to relax, and to practice!

Pathway 29

Give yourself a "sound massage."
Choose a phonetic sound you like— such as
"Ahhh...", "Ohhh...", or "Mmmmm."
Make this sound in a low tone.
It vibrates the torso.
Raise it a pitch; and it vibrates around the heart.
Hum it higher; and it vibrates
around the nose and roof of the mouth.
Each tone sends
a soothing and energizing message
to the brain!

30 Awesome Beauty

 I spent a long time in the hospital.

When I first walked outdoors after my discharge, I experienced an intensity of seeing and sensing. The grass seemed to shine like emeralds. The fresh air was euphoric. I felt like a child seeing everything for the first time! Previously I had taken the natural world for granted, rushing by on what I considered more important tasks. Suddenly I found myself in the present moment, experiencing the awesome beauty of everything.

Did this intense new love of nature and people have to do with the sensory deprivation I had experienced in the hospital? Or was it because I had seemed to lose everything familiar to me as a result of my surgery?

Sometimes when we are saying goodbye to something, we realize how precious it is. ∎

Pathway 30

*Try to be fully
in the present moment.
Focus on someone, or something,
and let everything else go.
Just appreciate
what you are focusing on in your mind and heart.*

31 Savoring the Taste

I went to my parents' home for a few weeks after leaving the hospital. They concocted interesting blender food recipes, entertained me royally, and generally made me feel at home.

I craved fruits and vegetables, and felt distaste for coffee and fatty meats. The coffee upset my stomach, and some meats were impossible to chew with half my face paralyzed. When I did get meat down, it felt heavy on my stomach.

I began to savor the taste of fresh vegetables, the richness of grains, and the sweetness of real fruit.

And water, cold spring water, became my #1 beverage. It went down pure and cool.

I also wanted "comfort foods" that I associated with good times in my life— such as Canadian bacon and an omelet. ∎

Pathway 31

*Be grateful for and
savor the taste of food
as you eat it slowly.
This can enhance
the quality of the experience
and help you to feel better!*

32 Housewalking

My family and friends took me for drives along back country roads, and we walked in the woods. I loved the smell of the pine trees, the songs of birds, and the sight and sound of clear water falling over rocks. It was a great setting for practicing my walking.

On days when the weather wouldn't permit me to go outdoors, I did housewalking. I created a walking track which went from room to room in the house. Sometimes I found myself circling around a small room, doing a figure-eight between pieces of furniture, walking down a hall or up a flight of stairs.

It didn't matter as long as it created a continuous track. I put on my favorite music and walked, accompanied by the sound. I never walked very quickly; but it was healthy movement of the whole body. ∎

Pathway 32

Try housewalking.
Or,
when you don't feel capable
of getting out of bed,
create an imaginary track
in whatever setting you would like,
and walk it in your mind!

33 Acute Pain

After two weeks at my parents' home, I was back in the hospital for further surgery— to cut the nerve feeding the left side of my tongue so that it could be hooked to the nerve that fed the left side of my face. The neurosurgeon felt that this procedure would bring my face back to more normal functioning and appearance. The surgery went well, and I was taken immediately to a ward room rather than the Intensive Care Unit. After a few days I was sitting up, eating and walking.

On the fourth day, however, something happened. I experienced an acute attack of muscle spasms in my face and neck. I thought I would die of the pain.

This happened on a weekend, and my doctor was not available. So a doctor from the emergency department came to my room, and after much consultation about my situation he gave me a shot which put me to sleep. When I woke up the pain was gone, and it never returned. I can only speculate that it was caused by the change-over of nerve impulses from the facial nerve to the tongue nerve. ∎

Pathway 33

Sometimes when I am feeling rough, I communicate four things to the part of my body which is in discomfort: Compassion; Love; Appreciation; and (I Picture) wellness.

*I call this message to my body: **"CLAP."***

1. *"C" is for Compassion. Compassion means "to feel with." So I say words or send thoughts such as, "I am sorry for what you are going through." Sometimes I am more specific, such as, "I am sorry you broke a bone when we fell on the ice."*

2. *"L" is for Love. I send love in the form of unconditional acceptance to the area of my body that is not well. I say or think, for example: "I send you love." Or just, "I love you." Feel it!*

3. *"A" is for Appreciation. Appreciation is gratefulness. I say and send thoughts such as, "I appreciate you! I appreciate your strength in bearing this pain, and for all the ways you have helped me in my life." It helps to think of specific examples of your appreciation, and to express them.*

4. *"P" is for Picturing. Picture wellness and wholeness. I think and say such things as: "I am picturing you in front of me, and see you well and whole. My mind remembers how it was when we were well."* *

Practice "CLAP" when you are feeling well, so that you will be better able to do it when you are in discomfort.

34
Sick Days

It was immediately after the acute pain attack after my nerve surgery that I began to experience episodes of head pressure, high fever and vomiting. These seizures hit me every few weeks, and wiped out an entire day each time. The symptoms usually started early in the morning, and lasted about ten hours, at which time it seemed like someone inside my head threw a switch, and the pressure, fever and vomiting clicked off. One minute I would feel deathly sick. The next minute I felt fine, and was ravenously hungry. The neurosurgeon thought that these episodes were related to a sensory nerve being caught in scar tissue.

Whatever the cause, I went deep within myself to try to figure out what to do about this, since no medication seemed to help me. I learned a lot about

34

healing due to these "sick days," because I was always asking myself, "What will help me to feel better?"

Years later, after having to go to a hospital emergency room in a dehydrated condition following a 3-day vomiting episode, my brother-in-law sent me an audiotape relaxation program, designed by the Northwestern University Medical School to help epileptics control seizures. In several weeks I was able to commit this relaxation process to memory. I could do it whenever I had even several free minutes during a day, no matter where I was.

Combined with taking an Ergotomine medication, this process has virtually removed the previous "sick days" from my life! Neither the

34

medication nor the relaxation process are effective for me by themselves, but when combined at the first sign of head pressure, they stop the head pain and vomiting almost immediately. It has given me back much of my life!

"Anatomy Breathing" (described in the Appendix, page 177), is a modification of the Northwestern University relaxation program. I have added to it information about how certain muscles move to relax, since being able to visualize this process makes it more real for me. ∎

Pathway 34

Allow your attention
to flow from one muscle group
in your body
to another.
Take deep breaths,
and as you breathe out
tell the muscles in each body part
to relax.
Visualize and feel them doing so.

35 Down-Slide

I continued to recuperate at my parents' home. They were so supportive—like two angels in a dark night.

I was dealing with tremendous losses. Gone were my health, job, home, physical appearance, even normal bodily functions. I wrote in my journal one day, "I feel depressed because of all I have to give up, and anxious about 'Whatever will I do? Where will I go?' It's hard to watch my meaning and independence slip through my fingers like sand. Giving up the keys to my apartment are my last reminder of that."

35

Later I wrote, "I need to let go and accept life as it is, and do what I can."

Then a renewed sense of depression would hit me like a tidal wave. And I began to feel angry. I wanted to blame something, or someone, for my brain tumor and all I had been through. I wrote, "I feel anger rising in me, anger I can't even express, because it would deeply hurt people whom I want to direct it toward. So I'll keep it all inside, and let it hurt me! How much do I think of myself ... putting myself through this?"

35

I was saved from my overwhelming depression and anger by flowers... walking in the park... reading good books... prayers... non-resistance... eating delicious food... anti-stress vitamins (B-complex, C & E)... talking things out... writing in my journal... and getting enough sleep! ∎

Pathway 35

*When you don't feel well,
remember to be good to yourself.
Think of
as many nurturing things
as you can
to do for yourself!*

36 Forgiveness Letters

Once when I was feeling depressed, a friend suggested that I search my mind for someone I hadn't forgiven.

Then he said, "Write a letter to that person telling them how you really feel. You don't have to send the letter if you don't want to. Then write another letter representing that person's reply to your letter to them."

This "letter writing" has helped sensitize me to other people's perspectives, and resulted in my being a more forgiving, loving person. Then I feel better! ∎

Pathway 36

The Greek word αφiomae means "to let go."
It also means "to forgive."
So I feel better when I practice letting go
—forgiving—
if I feel hurt, frustrated
or bothered by something.
It's not always easy.
But a forgiveness letter helps
to resolve feelings
and gain perspective.

37 A Crystal House

About this time I had a dream about building a "crystal house." It was in the woods, by water, with sunlight shining upon it. Certain crystals intensify light and energy, and this seemed to be happening with the crystal house.

In my dream I invited a woman in need of healing to come into my crystal house and lie down on a soft couch. Before she entered the house she was met and hugged by a group of people —past and present acquaintances— who loved and cared about her. These people then joined hands around the house and "beamed" their combined love and appreciation and healing intention toward the woman as she lay on the couch inside.

When I awoke from the dream, I thought how wonderful it would be to have the money and know-how to build such a house. Then I realized that I could build such a house in my mind— to help me feel better. ■

Pathway 37

1. Get comfortable, close your eyes, relax your muscles, and concentrate on your breathing.
2. Picture a scene in the woods, near water, where the sun is shining on a "crystal house."
3. See dear friends and family—past and present—come up to you, look at you with appreciation, tell you how much they love you, and give you a hug. Feel the warm hugs!
4. Then walk into the crystal house and lie down on the soft couch. See the rainbows of color being made by the sun shining through the crystal walls of the house. Feel the warmth of the sunlight coming through the walls, and the support of your loved ones outside who have joined hands and are beaming love and healing intention toward you. Maybe you can intuitively "hear" some of them sending their good thoughts to you, telling you how much they love and appreciate you. Stay there as long as you want to, savoring the light and love coming to you!

38
Slow
Flow

Even though it was difficult for me to walk, I wanted to exercise in some manner. Fortunately, I had taken Yoga classes taught by my friend, Mollie Sinclair, back in the 1960's, so I was able to draw upon what I remembered from my yoga training. I also reviewed several yoga books to improvise an exercise program I could do, whether I was in bed, or sitting in a chair or on the floor.

I call my routine *Slow Flow*, and have described this program in the Appendix (page 180). ∎

Pathway 38

Do some form of movement
that you enjoy
while lying in bed,
sitting on the edge of the bed,
in a chair, or
on the floor.

39
Rainbow Man

About six weeks after I was out of the hospital, my father took me to get a new prescription for my glasses. My surgery had actually improved the sight in my left eye, resulting in a need for new glasses. The optometrist we went to see was a friend of my father's from a local men's service club connection. When we walked into the office my father and the optometrist began chatting, and in the course of their conversation the optometrist asked Dad if he had heard about what

39

happened to a mutual acquaintance in the service organization. "A few months ago he had a heart attack—and he had a miraculous recovery." My father replied, "Oh, yes, I know about that. He was in the hospital in a bed near Mary in the Intensive Care Unit."

I wondered if this was the same man I had seen when I experienced myself "floating" on the ceiling of the Intensive Care Unit. But I said nothing to anyone about the possibility that this man might be the one I saw the

39

rainbow arch down and touch, causing him to immediately sit up. I was having a difficult enough time with the physical struggles of learning to walk and talk and eat, and I couldn't handle people thinking I had gone crazy on top of everything else! ■

Pathway 39

*Our thoughts
are an energy
that may connect us with others.
If we think about someone else
with thoughts of love and healing,
or conversely, anger or anxiety,
we send them that kind of energy!
Send thoughts
of love and appreciation.
Others will feel better—
and you will too!*

40 Pendle Hill

Before I learned I had a brain tumor I had planned to spend my three weeks' vacation plus two weeks of annual study-leave at Pendle Hill, a Quaker Center for Study and Contemplation in Pennsylvania. I had been attracted to the Quakers from the first time I had visited a Friends Meeting for Worship.

Now, in the summer of 1982, a renowned author and priest, Henri Nouwen, would be leading a conference at Pendle Hill on ministry. I had read two of his books, *Genesee Diary* and *The Wounded Healer*, been much helped by them, and looked forward to the opportunity of learning from Henri and others over a five-week period.

40

In the meantime, I had learned about my tumor and undergone surgery, with its debilitating effects. Should I still try to go to Pendle Hill as previously planned, I wondered? From all I had read about Pendle Hill, it sounded like a very quiet, healing place. So even though I could hardly keep my balance, I decided to go. The conference turned out to be a high point of my life: stimulating, creative ideas, a beautiful setting, and loving, supportive people.

I went to Pendle Hill for five weeks, and stayed for two years! The experience was one of living simply and quietly, sleeping long hours, worshipping in silence every morning, eating delicious, healthy food, walking, and reading

40

everything, from a book about Quantum Physics to one on Foot Reflexology. I made pottery in the Pendle Hill pottery shop, sorted used clothes to send to a mission, did Re-evaluation Counseling, had fun with friends, hooked a rug, kept a journal, and even wrote a book manuscript! I learned to do calligraphy, devised some stress relief suggestions, wrote music, shared in the work of the community— and fell in love!

These two years at Pendle Hill turned out to be an incomparable "feel-better" experience for me! ∎

Pathway 40

*When feeling lost,
not knowing which way to turn,
go to places that resonate
with what is most authentically YOU.
Take hold of fragments
of feel-good memories from your past,
and create courses of action
in the present that feel like
they would enhance your life!*

41 Follow Your Passion

I asked a friend of mine who is a nurse and wellness counselor what, in her opinion, was the most healing thing I could do for myself. She said, "Follow your passion!"

I have since asked a number of people what they are passionate about. Many people just look at me quizzically and say, "I don't know!"

Here are some questions that have helped me get in touch with what I am passionate about:

1. What did you feel passionate about when you were a child?
2. What was it about your childhood passion that you enjoyed the most?
3. Think of someone close to you whom you looked up to. What was their greatest positive strength?
4. Think of moments in your life when you felt most alive and happy. What were you doing then?
5. What personal quality do you wish each of your parents would have had if it had been possible?

41

6. If there were no restrictions on your life, what would you most like to do now?

7. If you knew this was the last day of your life, and you could live it any way you wanted to, what would you do?

The answers to these questions will probably suggest what you are passionate about. Reflect on your answers and play with them. Gradually, or suddenly, your inner guidance will make your passion clear. Then: *follow your passion!*

Begin by taking a first step in that direction today! The first five minutes can be the most difficult in moving in a new direction. But if we spend five minutes on a new activity, we're often up and going, and want to keep on going! ∎

Pathway 41

Follow Your Passion!

42 Lawn Mowing

Journal entry from my first fall at Pendle Hill: October 7, 1982

It feels good to slow down my life so that I can keep up with it! My windows are open wide to the warmth here at Pendle Hill. There's sunlight in the treewood, fire and shine in every leaf, and a soft green silence. I can almost hear the dew falling!

I saw a man out last evening mowing his lawn. It caused me to stop and reflect on what is important and meaningful in life. The man seemed to be enjoying what he was doing.

42

What is important and meaningful, of course, is different for each of us. On these autumn days, I've been picking up colorful fallen leaves and moving them to well-traveled pathways so that their beauty might be noticed by more people. This is my "lawn mowing"!

I feel a simplicity of living here. When the noise stops, I can hear my inner music.

During the autumn months of 1982, I saw fall come in a new way. I watched

42

the leaves change color each day; and I went for long walks, kicking my feet through the leaves.

Nature attracted me because of its slower, gentler vibrations, and it was often easier for me to be with a tree than a person. ■

Pathway 42

*Take a ten-minute walk
in natural surroundings.
Receive what nature is giving to you—
lightness of air,
rustle of leaves,
calming of wind,
rhythm of water,
sight of stars.*

43 Calm Cards

I began creating "Calm Cards" to use at times when I needed practical suggestions to relieve stress. (I wished that I had had these cards during the long days I was in the hospital following surgery!)

"Calm Cards" is now a pack of 36 cards containing a variety of mental and physical stress relief suggestions. They are handy because they can be carried in a pocket or purse and used at free moments when one feels under tension. Following are a few Calm Card stress relief suggestions. ■

Pathway 43

When your thoughts
feel scattered,
bring your thinking
back to a place
behind the center
of your forehead.

Quantum physics tells us
that an observer changes
the thing observed—
down to the minutest atom.
Stand back and observe:
look at whatever is happening
in your life right now.
Just watch what is happening,
like an objective observer,
without getting caught up
in the "drama."

When you feel yourself becoming
either "hyper" or depressed,
recognize that a big "high" may
be followed by a big "low"
and vice versa.
Bring yourself back
to a more balanced place
by eating a balanced diet,
getting a good night's sleep,
taking some exercise —
and expressing caring
to someone!

Imagine breathing in
a stream of light
from your toes to your head —
and then breathe out
from head to toe.
Allow your jaw
and shoulders
to relax.

44 Firbank Field

 On November 1, 1981, I wrote in my journal:

Last night I slept out in Firbank Field with my friends, Caroline and Roger. It was All Saints Day and we talked about some of the saints in our lives— not the usual list of saints, but wonderful people who have affected our lives, like particular family members, friends or teachers.

We slept some of the time, talked a lot, and watched a full moon sail across the sky as Orion marched into the trees.

Pathway 44

*Have fun
with friends
in whatever way
is fun for you—
and
feel better!*

45
Journaling

One evening while talking with some friends I mentioned the painful head pressure that I sometimes had upon waking in the morning. My friend Bob suggested that if I got up for twenty minutes during the night it might help my blood circulation, clear away toxins in my body, and alleviate the morning head pressure.

I decided to try it. Waking up at about 2 a.m., I sat in an easy chair— and wondered what to do while sitting in the dark! There was a night-light in the room, and a notebook and pen sat on the small table beside my chair. So I decided to do some journal writing.

I had recently read a book by Morton Kelsey about journaling. He suggested journaling in the middle of the night in the form of a flow of

45

consciousness, putting down on paper whatever falls out of your mind! He feels that the unconscious is more awake at night and would express itself well on paper during those hours. He suggested beginning the journaling by either asking a question, or starting a conversation. I decided to try this, and the following was my first night's journal entry:

Question: "Is anyone there? Because I am too tired to think!"

Answer: "We are here. Stay asleep in your cloud and let us write it up. We meet you in the timeless, and joy in your being and becoming. You are growing up, and one day you will grow far enough to become a simple child. Wait for it! Anticipate the joy and wonder. It will come. Love

45

is the fuel to spark your energy. Let it come. Let us rest in you, and you in us."

Except for a vague memory, I didn't realize until the next morning what had been written in the night. It was not in my usual handwriting but in a lazy, sloppy hand— though intelligible enough that I could decipher it. I don't know if getting up in the night helped stave off my head pressure. But I got up many nights after that and wrote because of the interesting results of my first night's experience. Sometimes there was a message; and sometimes just incoherent, half-finished sentences. I didn't feel like sharing these messages with others, because they seemed personal. Often the words were a treasure of encouragement and wisdom to me, and I appreciated their flowing into the fabric of my life. ■

Pathway 45

*Journal at night!
Write down
what comes into
your mind.*

46
Friends

Sometimes when I awoke in the morning feeling sick, I called my friend Louise to come and sit with me. This wonderful person just dropped whatever she was doing and came to my room. She would sit in a chair by my bed, content to just sit... or talk... or listen. I would find myself beginning to talk with her, and it was a real pain therapy for me. We talked about things that had happened in our past, or shared recent happenings. Or I sometimes just lay there with my eyes closed, knowing that she was there, and not feeling that I needed to respond to anything. After a while she would leave. But the "feeling better" part stayed with me. ∎

Pathway 46

*Ask a friend
who is caring and non-judgemental
to come for a visit.*

47 A Healing Cabin

The following is a visualization process that helps me feel better!

In trying to alleviate some of the side effects of my brain surgery, I was sent to a large medical clinic for biofeedback training. There they asked me to think of images of healing things. The doctor was able to measure the effect of each image on my body. Eventually I had generated a collection of particularly healing images— which I wove together in a visualization of a "healing cabin." In the scene was a cozy log cabin in a green woods, a comfortable blue chair, flowers, a white cat, a fire in the fireplace, and the sound of a nearby waterfall. Your healing cabin, of course, can incorporate any elements that are calming and relaxing for you.

Close your eyes, and pay attention to your breathing for a moment, feeling the air as it passes in and out of your nostrils. Now visualize walking along a path through a woods, allowing your senses to experience your surroundings— such as smelling the scent of pine, feeling a warm light breeze brushing your face, seeing the lovely shimmer of green trees, or hearing woodland sounds.

As you walk along the path you see a cozy log cabin nestled in the trees. You sense that this is a healing cabin, and you walk toward it. As you step onto the front porch, a low door is opened from the inside by a healing person in your life. This person might be a close friend, family member, divine being, healing angel— or even a cartoon character. This healing individual invites you in, and gives you a hug. Feel the warmth of the hug. You might talk with this person— or say nothing. See what happens.

A friendly cat runs up to you, so you sit in a comfortable chair by the fireplace and invite the cat to curl up on your lap. The cat purrs and settles down to sleep. (If you don't like cats, try a cuddly little lap dog!)

You are wonderfully warmed by the fire in the fireplace, and become aware of the soothing sounds of a

47

waterfall wafting through one of the cabin windows. Some lovely flowers fill a vase on the fireplace mantle.

Now relax in the cabin, staying as long as you want. Then count from 5 to 1 to bring yourself back up to a normal waking state.

Sometimes when I am in the healing cabin, I imagine a white screen on the cabin wall as I sit in the comfortable chair by the fireplace. Then I visualize *myself* on the screen - or anyone else I want to send feel-better thoughts to. There is a jar of healing green salve on the table next to my chair, and I rub some of the salve on the image of myself (or another), gently working it into areas that are painful, or don't feel well.

One nice thing about this miraculous green salve is that you can visualize, even feel, it penetrating right into your muscles, bones, and other body parts. In the altered dimension of your imagination, there are no barriers or limits! ■

Pathway 47

*It seems to me
that when I visualize or talk
about something peaceful or pleasant,
my body relaxes.
In a state of relaxation,
blood can circulate more freely—
bringing oxygen
and nutrients
to the cells.*

48
Hypnosis

Because I was feeling fearful about the high fever and vomiting days that I was experiencing, I wrote out a feel-better affirmation, and went to see a hypnotist. Under hypnosis, he repeated my feel-better affirmation to me, and it helped me to live fully in spite of my apprehension. ■

Pathway 48

*If you choose
to employ
a hypnotist
in your feel-better program,
write out
a feel-better affirmation
and ask the hypnotist
to repeat it to you
while you are in
light hypnosis.*

49 Quaker Meeting

It was a typical morning at Pendle Hill. I heard the bell sounding, almost like an ancient cathedral bell. Fifteen minutes until Meeting for Worship. I rose quickly from my narrow bed and looked around in wonder at my cozy room on the second floor of the barn. The rug I was hooking added a splash of color to the desk in one corner. An orange balloon was helium-stuck to the wall. It said, "Happy Birthday, Mary." And my shamrock plant beamed from its place on the window sill.

Because it was cold, I hurriedly put on some warm clothes. I groped my way to the bathroom. Then downstairs to the first floor of the barn, where Meeting was held.

The first thing that enveloped me upon entering the meeting room was a warm, pulsing silence. All the prayers of over 50 years of

49

daily Meeting had distilled there as a special energy that was like a warm, embracing hug.

I sat in my usual place on a wooden bench by the entrance door. Sunlight was sifting in the east windows, creating a sea of green light where it filtered through plants. I took a deep breath and began to relax into the quiet— only stirring slightly at the sound of the creaking boards as someone crossed the room and settled in on a facing bench.

As I gradually became still, I was aware of tensions in my body, and incessant chatter going on in my mind. So I breathed out "through" those tense places, and let go of as much chatter as I could right then. The chatter returned and I let it go again on another breath!

I looked at the gathered faces: some were rugged; some had an expression of perplexity, and

49

others of peace. There was a simple beauty everywhere as we sat and shared equally in the silence. We come to Meeting with the belief that there is that of the Divine in everyone, and we sit in silence with a desire to draw near to that Spirit and to each other.

I closed my eyes and let my breath take my attention into my inner body, I felt a subtle energy of being that pervaded every cell and stretched to my toes. Sometimes I focused on an image, a feeling, or a word such as "calm."

In the next hour someone, or several persons, might feel moved by the Spirit to speak. And in some Meetings, no one spoke. Either can be a gift.

Then the bench I was sitting on began shaking like a great heart, and I knew that the person next to me was about to speak. She stood up and her words cut the silence.

"A Friends' Meeting in Quebec was trying to organize a bilingual Meeting for Worship. They decided to have a half-hour of silence in French, followed by a half-hour in English! My question is, 'What language can we bring?'" My bench-neighbor sat down. The silence continued flowing until an older gentleman rose from his place on the far side of the Meeting room:

"I asked God, 'What's the answer to life?' God said, 'What's the question?' I said, 'The questions is, 'What's the answer?' And God said, 'The answer is love!'"

Again— silence. And then I heard a message inside my head followed by a voice that said, "You don't want to speak. It will sound stupid to all these

49

people. You'll probably forget half of what you want to say and it won't come out right." I started to shake, and my heart raced. I knew my heart would pound in my body until I spoke the message. The words were almost pushed out of my mouth.

"My silences have been invaded by a Mockingbird this week. I laugh when I hear her trill a series of bird songs.

"Then I know a moment of sadness as I think, Will she ever sing her own song?"

In the quiet space that followed we sat, open to the Divine presence. Then the hand of my bench-neighbor touched mine, and as others touched their neighbors, the Meeting drew to a close. I opened my eyes and everything seemed to shine with a clear light.

■

Pathway 49

*Allow your breathing
to take your attention
into your inner body.
Feel your abdomen expanding
and contracting as you breath.
Visualize yourself surrounded
by light. Breathe in light, and
as you breathe out, feel the light
and your connectedness
with all Being.*

50 The Blue Liquid

Here's a process that a Roman Catholic nun taught me. It sometimes helps to relieve pain. And for the times it works, it's worth trying!

She said, "If pain needs calming, first picture the 'shape' of the pain. Then imagine this shape is a container. Next fill the container with imaginary blue liquid. Ask, 'What is happening to the blue liquid now?' Keep asking and answering this question until the blue liquid drains out of the container."

At this point I often find that the pain is gone.

Pathway 50

Employ your imagination as a tool in pain management.

51
Making Lists

 In January, 1983, I wrote in my journal:

Darn! I forgot again to take the clothes out of the washer and put them in the dryer. I invariably forget practical things. I am sort of floating through my life and focused only on what is present now. What happened to the person that I used to be— so vital and alive and into doing? Right now I am content to just float and be. But it irritates me when I forget the clothes!

When I became aware of how "floaty" I was, I started making lists to remind myself of the practical things that I needed to remember to do to support my everyday life. Routines were grounding for me. Exercise and eating brought me into my body. As did an occasional sip of Bailey's Irish Cream in coffee! Sometimes I felt a shift in consciousness and I thought, "I'm here. I'm really here!"

It helped me to go beyond resistance to doing chores, to revel in the chore and dive in deeply.

Pathway 51

*Complete
a project or chore
which is undone.
It feels good
to cross chores off your list.
The most difficult part
is the first five minutes
of getting started!*

52 Hands-On Help

Some file folders were on the shelf of my closet, just beyond reach. I wanted to get them down, so I dragged my desk chair over to the closet and carefully climbed up. My balance was still precarious; I never knew when it was going to be there for me. Suddenly I was falling, arching backward. I landed hard on the floor. The internal chatter began, "My God, what have I done?"

I didn't move, but mentally began clicking through my memory for what to do next. I had recently taken a few courses in hands-on methods to help me feel better. Surely there was something I had learned that might help.

As I lay there on my back, I carefully slid my hands under my back to where the adrenal glands are located, just above the waistline. As I rested on my hands, I felt the warm energy from my palms going to the adrenal area. I mentally recalled and pictured the moment of falling, took a deep breath, and let go of as much of this traumatic event as I could at that moment. I let it go with the breath and continued doing this for several minutes.

I felt calmer then, and more relaxed. I slowly attempted to roll over and get up. Wincing a bit as I put some weight on my left foot, I lifted myself onto the bed and lay there while I knocked on the wall to send an S.O.S. signal to Bruce, who occupied the room next to mine. Thankfully, he was there and almost immediately knocked on my door. I explained the situation and asked if he would please get me some

52

ice to put on my ankle, which was hurting. He returned within minutes with a bag of ice from the main kitchen. He packed the ice around my ankle, and bundled a blanket around it. I settled down and dozed off.

When I woke up, the weight on my ankle reminded me of my fall, and I gingerly extracted myself from the blanket and ice bag. I gently got on my feet, and heaved a sigh of relief when I felt no pain. ∎

Pathway 52

*Placing your hands
over the adrenal gland area,
palm side to skin on the back above the waist
for a few minutes,
can help in the feel-better process.
Picture a traumatic event,
take a deep breath,
and let go
of as much trauma
as you can.*

53 Sadsbury Silence

 In April, 1983, I wrote in my journal:

I am on silent retreat at Sadsbury, a 250-year-old Quaker Meeting House in the Amish country of Pennsylvania. I find a space in a pine-scented corner near a window and roll out my sleeping bag. I settle in and spread a few belongings, my paints and a journal. I didn't bring much with me. And it feels freeing.

Sadsbury Meeting House is located in the middle of a cemetery. I used to spook myself as a kid thinking what it might be like to walk through a graveyard at night. Now here I am sleeping in one! It is surprisingly comforting!

At sunset, walking outside, the azaleas and bronze elm are rich in color. I hug an old, fat tree. Then I follow a path to the stone wall of an Amish farm. There are cows grazing in the field. They look

53

at me curiously. Some move towards each other. I wonder if they are friends?

Sitting on the front porch and watching fog cloud in, I feel the "cloud of witnesses," the communion of saints, Sadsbury saints. The grave markers here hint at so many life stories: a boy who died at nineteen... a woman whose middle name is Axe... a rustic stone which declared, "Old soldiers never die"... a little grave marker for Lizzie... a tall rocket-like stone for Tom. Someone named "Islam" is dead. I see stones for "Father" and "Mother." My mother and father will be passing sometime. Can I accept this? Can I accept the passing of myself? Do I in all my energy of Being, realize that I am eternal and connected to all?

After a night of deep sleep, an irate jay wakes

53

me at dawn— or is it the sun slanting in through the windows? I can see the light shining through the "V" of a bending black oak. The tree branches look like a widening way to the future. Dressing quickly and cutting a grapefruit for breakfast, I take it outside and sit on the porch in the warm sun. When the first grapefruit section goes down my throat, I taste a cold tang inside and out.

A song comes into my mind, and I hastily take my journal notebook from my pocket and jot down the notes of the song on makeshift scales. Sometime I will translate these notes into music.

When I wakened in this old Meeting House, I realized that everything I do is sacred— sleeping... waking... exercising... breathing... eating. These are sacred rituals.

A siren sounds and reminds me that life is "out there" also. I feel a closeness with others at a deeper level— and connected with all life. ∎

Pathway 53

*Quiet
the sounds
and
allow the senses
to give you
their gifts
in a more intense way.*

54
Creative Choices

My journal continues...

Creative choices are spread out like a smorgasbord before me at Pendle Hill. One thing on the menu is the ancient art of Calligraphy. It appeals to my love of creating beauty. Take the letters of the alphabet and push them around with a calligraphy pen until the form is pleasing. Then it's just a matter of practice. So I doodle calligraphy at odd moments. I also pen poems in ancient text, and write letters home in impressive script! It's not difficult as there are only twenty-six letters to decide about— how you want to form them on paper. Then it's just a matter of taking up a flat-tipped pen and pushing off!

My feast also includes puttering in the pottery shop, just mucking around and making wondrous creations. I get lost in time, molding the clay. My latest work of art is a free-form whimsical donkey for a Christmas crèche set. Someone walking through the pottery shop stopped and asked, "What's it like to drop out of the real world?" My answer flew up from the potter's wheel, "For me, this *is* the real world!" ∎

Pathway 54

*Be involved
in a creative expression or hobby:
painting... woodwork... cooking... music...
whatever appeals to you.
This can bring your life back
to a feel-better place,
as well as
be absorbing and satisfying.*

55 Umbrella Plant

One day when I was feeling particularly down and could hardly crawl because of the pain and difficulty in balancing, I recall hanging onto my bed and maneuvering my way to the foot of it in an effort to head in the direction of the bathroom. In the process I happened to brush against an umbrella plant which was sitting by a window in my room. Suddenly, I felt better! I turned around in surprise, and put my hands near the plant's leaves. I could feel gentle waves of energy flowing into my hands. It seemed like the umbrella plant was sharing feel-better energy with me! ■

Pathway 55

1. Get into a relaxed position
near a flower, plant or tree.

2. Look at the plant
and appreciate its beauty.

3. Hold out your hands
with your palms toward petals,
leaves or tree bark.

4. After spending a few minutes with the plant,
talk to it mentally, or out loud—
thanking it for sharing its life energy with you!

56 Claim Divine Power

My friend Libby took me to a faith healing service at a nearby Episcopal church. At the altar rail the minister looked me in the eyes and said, "Claim the power of Jesus' name. As a child of God you are a complete, whole, Divine creature. Claim it!"

There is something very powerful in this process. You may want to put it in your own words— such as, "I claim the Divine power in my life!" Or "I affirm that every cell in my body is in perfect balance and working order." Then recall a time when you felt that way in your life. Feel it now!

Pathway 56

Claim Divine Power!

57 Dream Detective

After a day of severe head pressure and vomiting, I was looking for something to help me to feel better. I decided to ask for guidance in a dream. I wrote down my request for information on a note pad, and finally fell asleep. I dreamed that I was relaxing on a bed beside an open window. A fresh breeze was coming in the window, blowing a white curtain. The curtain became misty, and then took the shape of a ghost. The ghost was a man with deep lines in his face, who moaned in pain. I woke up with a feeling of horror.

In the morning when I awoke I analyzed the dream. It seemed to suggest the importance of relaxing, and of getting fresh air (oxygen). I interpreted the man's deep facial lines, and moans, as highlighting my head pain and the paralysis in the left side of my face. Our bodies have innate wisdom to share with us. One way to tune into that wisdom is through dreams. Anyone can learn to become a "dream detective," discovering meanings from the clues in their dream stories, and thus receiving personalized guidance. ■

A dream interpretation procedure is in the Appendix, page 192.

Pathway 57

*Our bodies have wisdom
to share with us.
One way to access that wisdom
is through dreams.*

58
Epilogue

In the Spring of 1984, I called a "Clearness Committee" meeting, a Friends/Quaker process for sorting out a situation or problem.* With the support and guidance of my Committee, I was empowered to take my next step. *I felt like I was jogging through space!*

---

* Refer to *Spiritual Discernment and the Use of Clearness Committees Among Friends*, Patricia Loring, Pendle Hill Pamphlet #305, available from the Pendle Hill Bookstore, 338 Plush Mill Road, Wallingford, PA 19086.

Pathway 58

Seek support and guidance from knowledgeable people.

59
David

It was through Clearness Committee guidance that I became Retreat Director at a Quaker retreat center in Ohio. I attended the local Quaker Meeting and it was there that I met my husband, David.

I fell in love with his twinkling Irish eyes, his enthusiasm, his inquisitive mind and caring ways.

Now, fifteen years later, I can say that David has taught me more than anyone about what it is to be a loving person.

We have experienced glorious adventures, survived health crises, enjoyed the company of family and friends, and learned a lot about healing and feel-better pathways.

David is a genius-level teacher. His former college students are continually telling me that he has changed their lives and opened new worlds to them. ■

Pathway 59

*A loving relationship
is a true feel-better experience in life.
Seek out relationships
where you feel affirmed and
appreciated for who you are,
listened to and cared for—
in the small loving acts
of everyday life.*

60 Postscript

During the week that my husband, David, finished proof-reading this manuscript, we had a telephone call from my Pendle Hill friend, Roger Conant. I had not seen Roger for fifteen years! He was calling to say that he was going to be in our area and would like to stop by and say hello.

When he came to visit, I told him about my book manuscript, *Jogging Through Space*, and asked his advice about how to get my hand-written manuscript into proper form to send to a publisher. Roger immediately offered to type it on his computer.

Roger and I have some major life experiences in common. Two years ago he was diagnosed with a brain tumor. He has spent several periods of time at Pendle Hill— including when I was there, and

60

also, during the last six months. He has a great interest in healing. Here is his inspiring story:

"Lying in bed one morning with my wife Shirley, a very strange feeling swept over me. I passed out, and Shirley reports that I had some sort of trembling convulsion. She called 911 and convinced me to go to the hospital, where they took CAT and MRI scans of my head, probably thinking I had had a stroke. No, it wasn't a stroke, and nobody has ever figured out what set off the original incident. But on the MRI they discovered that I had a brain tumor—fortunately a small one which could be operated on by a high-tech method called Stereotactic Radiosurgery, using beams of focused radiation rather than scalpels, and only a morning in the hospital rather than the sort of ordeal Mary had to

60

go through. *I researched this medical procedure on the Internet.* The operation to destroy the tumor seems to have been successful. The odd thing is, I never had any symptoms from the tumor. All the doctors are convinced that the original incident which sent me to the hospital was unrelated to the tumor, and nobody has any idea what caused that incident.

"I believe it was an intervention by the Great Spirit, sending me to the hospital so that the tumor could be discovered and treated while it was still small and not causing any trouble!

"However after the discovery of the tumor and before the successful treatment I naturally went through a tough time, not knowing if I would live, die, or be hopelessly disabled. To my surprise I found

60

this was a time of unusually rich spiritual life and happiness. The lessons I had learned earlier about living in the Now came back with great force, because when you seriously anticipate dying, the Now becomes really important! On my daily 15-mile bike ride to work along Lake Michigan I would marvel at the beauty of the early morning light and shadows, and at how great it was to be able to ride a bicycle. I would bend a finger and be amazed at how well it and the other body parts worked. I would eat a piece of toast and marvel at the flavors and texture, and at being able to swallow! Frozen puddles with lacy fingers of ice were gorgeous works of beauty. When the little green things started coming up in spring, each one was an inspiration. It was a time of endless appreciation, for What Is.

60

"The whole experience showed me that though suffering and pain and distress are always around and even inside us, so also there is, always around and inside us at all times and in all places, an endless field of small wonders of Life to be thankful for, if we can be open to them, indeed even notice them. And it has shown me that since Life can end at any time, it should be lived so that at all times, it is complete!" ■

Pathway 60

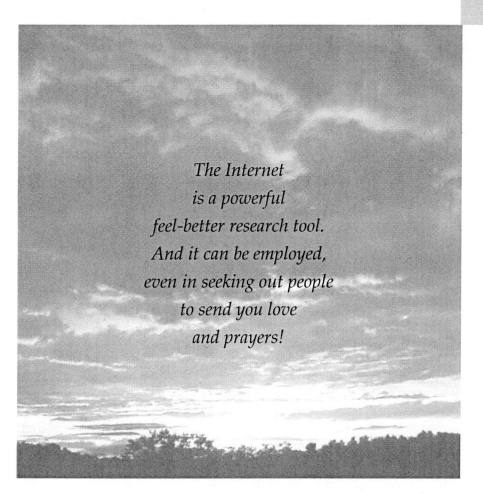

*The Internet
is a powerful
feel-better research tool.
And it can be employed,
even in seeking out people
to send you love
and prayers!*

Appendix

Self Massage
Anatomy Breathing
Slow Flow:
Bedexercises I & II
Copy Cats
Dream Detective

Self Massage

This can be done while sitting or lying down.

1. Place the middle 3 fingers of each hand on your chin. Begin to move the tips of these fingers in a circular motion as you move the fingers along the **jaw** line. Take a deep breath and tell your jaw to relax. This is an area where we carry a lot of tension. Cup your hands under your chin— spreading the fingers out toward the ears. Hold this position for a moment. Breathe deeply, and keep your mouth closed with each exhalation. Now, keeping your hands in this position, send love to your jaw and your entire head area while you breathe deeply for a minute— making the sound "Mmmm…" each time you breathe out. (I have found that it helps to send thoughts of love to each area of the body as you are massaging it. A way to remember to do this is to connect the sound "Mmmm…" with sending thoughts of love. These places are indicated by "Mmmm…" in the massage instructions.)

2. Moving now to your **neck**— where tension often resides, place the middle three fingers of both hands at the back of your neck where the skull and spine meet. Move your fingertips back and forth in this area for a minute.

3. Place the fingers of your right hand below the left ear. Knead the tips of the fingers firmly down the side of your neck and out to

Self Massage

the edge of your **shoulder**. Rub the shoulder area in a circular motion a few times. *Now with your left hand perform the same procedure on the right side of your neck and shoulder.*

4. Now, **hug yourself** with your right hand on the left side of your body, and your left hand on the right side. Hold this position for a minute while you take several deep breaths, exhaling through your nose with your mouth closed. Make the sound "Mmmm…" each time you breathe out. Make it a real hug— and feel love for yourself!

5. Next we move to the hand, and will massage the **left hand** first. Hold each finger in succession. Massage the top of that finger with your right thumb, making circular motions as you move from the nail all the way up the finger. Take your time with this. There is no hurry!

6. Now take the heel of your right hand and knead the back of the left hand on one side. Then repeat on the other half of the back of the left hand.

7. Resting the back of your left hand in your right hand, make circular motions in the palm of your left hand with your right thumb.

Self Massage

Gradually increase the size of the circles until they cover the entire palm of your hand.

8. Now hold your **left wrist** with your right hand for a minute. As you do so, take several deep breaths, exhaling through your nose. Make the sound "Mmmm..." each time you breathe out, and send thoughts of love to your hand/arm area.

9. Now, sweep your right palm up the entire length of your **left arm**. Do this motion several times, starting with the back of your arm and then moving to the sides and front of the arm. Next, resting your left arm close to your body, knead the arm with your right hand, moving up the left arm from hand to shoulder. Then lift your left arm up and knead the underside of the arm from hand to armpit— finishing by circling the armpit several times. *Now repeat steps 5-9 on your right hand and arm.*

10. Finally, **clasp your hands** and hold them **over your solar plexus**, and take several deep, relaxing breaths. Let go of as much tension as you can right now as you exhale. ∎

Anatomy Breathing

Here is a relaxation process I use 2-3 times a day!

When a muscle relaxes, it becomes either longer or wider, depending on the type of muscle. ***Anatomy Breathing*** is a process whereby you breathe out while directing your attention to a particular part of your body—for instance, your arm. As you breathe out, you tell the muscles in that body part to relax. Visualize and feel them do so. It's as if when you breathe out, a relaxing energy "swooshes" through the body part you are thinking about, with the muscles lengthening or widening depending on the type of muscle.

Everyone feels better when they receive loving attention. Your body parts are no exception. Allow your attention to flow from one muscle group to another with each out-breath. As a bonus, the muscle relaxation will allow more oxygen to nourish each area being relaxed.

I like to do *Anatomy Breathing* whenever I have a few free minutes (such as sitting in waiting rooms, in group meetings if I feel tension, or just before falling off to sleep at night). In the beginning, it may help to have someone else read the following instructions to you, or make a tape of your own voice reading them.

***Anatomy Breathing** is my modification of an audio-tape relaxation program produced by **The Relaxation Project**, Division of Psychology, Northwestern University Medical School, 303 E. Chicago, Chicago, IL 60611.*

Anatomy Breathing

The process:

Sit or lie down comfortably.

When you are ready, close your eyes.

Take a few deep breaths.

Relax.

Direct your attention to each of the body parts listed below, in the order given, breathing relaxation into the muscles as you allow them to lengthen or widen. Pause comfortably after each exhalation, picturing or feeling the relaxation flowing into the body part. You are the leader. Tell the muscles to follow and relax!

Go to these body parts and allow these muscle responses:

Hands	Lengthen	*Spine*	Move up from tailbone to neck, vertebra by vertebra
Wrists	Widen		
Arms	Lengthen	*Neck*	Lengthen & widen
Shoulders	Widen out	*Jaw*	Allow to hang loose
Chest	Lengthen & widen	*Mouth*	Allow the circle of muscles around your mouth to widen
Torso	Lengthen & widen		
Feet	Lengthen	*Cheeks*	Allow the muscles in your cheeks to widen
Ankles	Widen	*Eyes*	Allow the circle of muscles around your eyes to widen
Legs	Lengthen		
		Forehead	Widen & relax down

Anatomy Breathing

Take a deep breath and relax further.

Breathe deeper— and then deeper, experiencing a state of deep relaxation.

Say, *"Deeply relaxed."*

Now imagine yourself lying on a blanket at the beach. Visualize and feel the wet heat from the sand coming up through the blanket and penetrating the cells of your body, relaxing every cell. Feel this in your head, neck, back, and legs. Allow the sun's warmth to penetrate your face and the front of your body, warming the cells, relaxing the cells even more.

There is nothing for you to do but feel the wonderful feelings of relaxation flowing through your body. *Relax!*

When you are ready to come back to a normal waking state, count backwards from 5 to 1:

Five - Coming back.

Four - Feeling very refreshed.

Three - Breathe deeply.

Two - Now your eyes are open. Stretch!

One - Feeling fully awake, refreshed and alive! ■

Slow Flow

Three levels: do them in bed, sitting, or on the floor!

There are six words to remember while doing **Slow Flow**. After "Slow" and "Flow" come the words: **Visualize, Relax, Breathe, Love**. I remember these last four words with the memory aid, "VRBL" (pronounced verbal).

1. *Slow* - Move slowly through all movements, concentrating on what you are doing.

2. *Flow* - Make the movements flow gracefully. Go as far as you can with each movement without causing discomfort. If you feel pain, you've gone too far and need to ease off a bit.

3. *Visualize* - how you would like to do each exercise, holding that picture in your mind as you do it.

4. *Relax* - Say "Relax" during the exercises— to remind yourself to relax your jaws and joints (including hips).

5. *Breathe* - Breathe easily and naturally throughout each exercise. Don't hold your breath. Breathing brings nourishing oxygen to the muscles— helping them relax and become more movable.

6. *Love* - Send loving thoughts to your body.

After each exercise, relax for a few seconds to allow the stretched muscles to return to a resting position. Then "flow" into the next exercise.

Bedexercises I
Do these exercises on a firm mattress, or on the floor

Slow Flow

A. *Smile!* This is one of the most beneficial exercises there is. There are more muscles in the face than any other part of the body! Then pucker your lips. Alternate smiling and puckering 6 times. Remember the *Slow Flow* rules: slow; flow; visualize; relax; breathe; love.

B. *Pelvic Tilt*. This is an exercise that I learned from a physiotherapist to help strengthen my back and abdominal muscles.

   1. While lying on your back, pull your knees up until your feet are flat on the bed.

   2. Recall the rules for "Slow Flow" (Slow; Flow; VRBL), and while you implement these rules, tilt your pelvis up.

   3. Then allow the muscles to relax.

   4. Repeat the Pelvic Tilt 5 more times.

   5. End by strongly blowing air out of your mouth 3 times.

C. *Knee Bends* are excellent for stretching your legs and back.

   1. Lie on your back with both arms at your sides.

   2. Pull your knees up until your feet are flat on the bed.

   3. Now, raise your left knee up toward your chest while you bring your right hand up.

                                             Knee Bends continues…

Slow Flow

4. Place your right hand just below the left knee and pull to bring your knee even closer to your chest.

5. Then allow the left leg to move back to the bent-knee position with the foot resting on the bed.

6. Now do this movement with your right leg, assisted by your left hand.

Do these knee bends 6 times— alternating the left and right legs.

D. **Hand-to-Knees:** This is an isometric exercise that helps to strengthen the arms and legs.

1. Again, lie flat on your back with your knees bent so that your feet are flat on the bed.

2. Raise your left leg toward your chest— and at the same time place the heel of your left hand on your upper leg just above the knee.

3. Now push your hand against your leg with your leg resisting the push.

4. Then let your leg move back to the initial bent-knee position.

5. Do the same exercise with your right leg and hand.

Alternate the left and right leg and hand movements five more times. Then relax.

Slow Flow

E. ***Back Rock:*** Keeping in mind the ***Slow Flow*** instructions, bring your knees up toward your chest. Place your arms around your knees and lock your fingers together. From this position, rock back and forth like a rocking chair, 6 times. Relax.

F. ***Leg Raises***: This movement strengthens your legs and back.

1. Lie on your back with your hands at your sides, your right knee bent with your foot on the bed, and your left leg resting flat.

2. Recall the "Slow Flow" instructions.

3. Keeping your left leg straight, lift it as high as you comfortably can. Then let it slowly move back to the bed.

4. Repeat this 5 more times.

5. Then, do the same exercise with the right leg. Relax.

G. ***Raised Knee Bends:***

1. While lying on your back, raise your left thigh so it makes a 90° angle with the bed, keeping your knee bent.

2. Place your hands— one on each side of the thigh— just above the knee.

3. Now, recalling your "Slow Flow" instructions, raise the lower part of your left leg as far as you can.

Raised Knee Bends continues…

Slow Flow

4. Then let it flow back to its earlier position, making a 90° angle with your upraised thigh.

5. Continue this up-and-down knee bending until you have done it six times.

6. Now follow the same procedure for the right leg. Relax!

Bedexercises II
Do these exercises sitting on the edge of your bed, or in a chair.

A. ***Eye Exercises:*** I do a yoga exercise which has beneficial effects on my partially paralyzed face. It helps relax tense muscles, too.

1. Imagine a large clock facing you.

2. With your eyes open, move your eyes from one number to the next as you go clockwise from 1 to 12 around the clock.

3. Then reverse your eye movements, going counter-clockwise from 12 back to 1.

4. Repeat this clockwise/counterclockwise exercise 2 more times.

Slow Flow

B. *Eye Warmer* - Rub the palms of your hands together to warm them. Cover your eyes with your palms for one minute. Breathe deeply, and as you exhale, quietly make the sound, "Mmmm…" while sending love to your eyes, and remembering something peaceful.

This helps to relax the eyes and body. (Exercises that have helped my eyes tremendously are described by Dr. Wm. Bates, M.D., in a book first published in 1940, *Better Eyesight Without Glasses*, Holt, Rinehart and Winston, New York.)

C. *Neck Rolls*: This yoga exercise helps relieve tension and relax the entire body.

1. *Sit with your shoulders in a comfortable position.*

2. *Recall the "Slow Flow" instructions: slow; flow; visualize; relax; breathe; love.*

3. *Let your head drop slowly forward until it hangs limply like a rag-doll. Hold this position, breathing gently.*

4. *Bring your head up and, keeping your shoulders straight, gently allow your head to roll backwards — without straining.*

Neck Rolls continues…

Slow Flow

5. Bring your head upright.

6. Repeat this back-and-forth motion two more times.

7. Keeping your mouth closed, gently lean your head to the right while looking up.

8. Hold this position briefly. Then bring your head up and gently roll it to the left side.

9. Repeat this side-to-side motion two more times.

10. Let your head drop forward— again be rag-doll loose. Then gently roll it in a circular motion, first to the right, then back, then to the left, and forward again.

11. Having made a full circle, now roll your head in the opposite direction.

12. Repeat these two circles two more times.

D. **Knee Bends** (sitting): This exercise strengthens the legs and back.

1. While sitting up straight (shoulders back and down), with your legs dangling over the side of the bed, bend your left lower leg up as far as it will go. Remember to **Slow Flow**.

Slow Flow

2. *Hold your leg in this position for several seconds.*

3. *Then, let your leg flow back to its resting position.*

4. *Continue this up and down knee bend until you have completed six bends.*

5. *Now, follow the same procedure for the right leg.*

Relax! Now lie on your back on the bed for a few minutes to allow the stretched muscles to relax. Breathe normally and feel the relaxation flowing through your whole body.

Copy Cats
Do these exercises on the floor.

Cats are supple animals. They can arch and curl; stretch and flow; walk with grace; laze in deep restfulness; and take the fall. From ancient times, yogis have been copying the movements of cats.

A. ***Cat Crawl:*** This is our earliest method of getting around—crawling on the floor! It is great for strengthening arm and leg muscles.

1. *Crawl forward six knee-steps. Remember the **Slow Flow** instructions. Do this Cat Crawl slowly and think about each "knee*

Cat Crawl continues...

Slow Flow

step" as you are taking it. Breathe easily, allowing the motions to flow.

B. **Cat Sit:** This is similar to the yoga pose called "Japanese Sitting Position." It eases tension and improves circulation in the legs and feet.

1. Kneel in an upright position with your feet together and your toes pointing back.

2. Slowly lower your buttocks onto your heels.

2. Relax, placing your weight on your heels and keeping your back straight.

4. Put your hands on your thighs.

5. As you improve you will be able to point your toes together and let your heels fall apart. Nestle in this "seat"— sitting on your haunches like a cat!

C. **Cat Curl:** It feels so good to round oneself into a ball. Feel the tension leaving your body with this pose.

1. Kneel with your legs together.

Slow Flow

2. Rest your buttocks on your heels, and place the backs of your hands on the floor, fingers pointing backwards.

3. Lower your head slowly to the floor, sliding your hands gently backwards so that your arms end up beside your body.

4. Rest your head on the floor and relax completely with your chest against your knees.

5. Stay curled in this position for several minutes.

6. Then slowly raise your head, letting your hands come back to their previous position, until you are sitting on your haunches again.

D. *Cat Stretch:* Flow from Cat Curl to Cat Stretch. This exercise strengthens the back and arms, and gives a pleasant stretch to the entire body. It also tightens the chin area.

1. Kneel on all fours.

2. Rock slightly back first, and then lower your chest in a sweeping motion, trying to rest your "Adam's Apple" on the floor. Don't strain.

3. Hold this position for 5 seconds, with most of your weight on your arms.

Cat Stretch continues…

Slow Flow

4. *Return to the original position, and arch your back in an upward motion like an angry cat.*

5. *Hold for 5 seconds, and then relax.*

6. *Now, bring your right knee towards your head, touching your head if you can. (Simply go as far as you are able to.) Hold for 5 seconds.*

7. *Next, stretch your right leg back and up, keeping it straight. Hold. Keep the head up and arms straight.*

8. *Return the leg slowly to the head. Hold. Relax.*

9. *Now, repeat this process with your left leg.*

10. *Repeat the whole series once more.*

E **The Lion:** I love this yoga posture! It reduces tension, improves circulation, and even helps your complexion. It is known to help relieve sore throat, and improve the voice.

1. *In a kneeling position, sit on your heels with your hands on your thighs, palms down (Cat Sit).*

2. *Spread your fingers and slide them forward until the tips touch the floor.*

Slow Flow

3. Bend your body forward, bringing your buttocks off your heels and keeping your arms straight.

4. Open your eyes wide.

5. Stick out your tongue as far as it will go, as if you are going to touch your chin with the tip of your tongue.

6. Exhale your breath as you stick out your tongue.

7. Hold for several seconds.

8. Pull in your tongue and sit back on your heels. Relax.

9. Repeat twice more.

Relax

Lie on your bed, breathe normally, and relax!

∎

Dream Detective

The idea of asking for guidance in a dream is not new. In Middle Eastern countries, as far back as the 6th century B.C., trained personnel resided in hospital-like settings. People seeking dream guidance would come to such "hospitals" and prepare to have a dream by becoming quiet, and going through rituals- such as writing their question down on a clean linen bag, which was soaked in oil and set aflame as a lamp wick.

Here is a dream interpretation procedure:

1. Keep a writing pad and pen beside your bed.

2. Write down your dream question before you go to sleep, asking for a helpful dream that will answer your question.

3. When you awaken from a dream, lie still for a moment and replay the dream in your mind— even if it's only isolated images you can recall. Remembering dream stories and images is made easier by remaining in the body position you were in when you awakened from the dream— or moving back to that position if you change it upon waking.

4. Because dreams are easily forgotten, record your dream images as soon as possible. If there were unusual names or spoken

Dream Detective

words in the dream, write them down first since they may be forgotten more quickly than the dream story itself. If I awaken in the night with a dream, I record key words to trigger my memory of the dream in the morning.

5. A night light can help you see to write if you awaken in the night with a dream. Be sure your note paper is big enough so that you don't write words on top of other words in the darkness!

6. In the morning or on a day off, set aside some quiet moments to write out your dream. I write the dream in the present tense rather than the past, since it makes the dream story more immediate and alive.

Next comes the fun of interpreting the dream. Here are some ideas that have helped me:

1. Give the dream a title. This helps identify the main meaning or messages of the dream.

2. Pay attention to the first sentence of your dream story; it may be a major clue to the message of the dream.

3. Underline key words in the dream. Then make a list of these key words, followed by a word that you associate with each key

Dream Detective

word. Then rewrite the dream, substituting your associated words for the underlined key words. Often a whole new understanding of the dream appears.

4. Talk the dream over with someone. My friends and I enjoy sharing our dreams with each other, and talking about different "levels" of interpretation. Often another person will see symbolic meanings and messages that you have failed to notice. A group of several friends can shed light on a dream if each person interprets the dream as if it were their own dream (i.e. "If this were my dream..."). Also, there are many good "dream dictionaries" that explain universal dream symbols.

5. If you would like to go more deeply into the meaning of a dream, pick out one of the major characters in the dream and have a "conversation" with him or her (or even an important animal, or object, in the dream). Write down a question you wish to ask the dream character, and record their response— continuing the conversation until it ends.

I once had a dream where a very threatening person was in the basement of a church. But when I talked with him in an imaginary conversation after I awoke, I realized that he had tried to

Dream Detective

scare me just because he wanted to get my attention about a problem that was highlighted in the dream. When I understood this, he was no longer a threatening person, but instead gave me some good advice in my "conversation" with him! At some level, every character in the dream is an aspect of yourself trying to say something to you. Thank these dream characters for trying to help you!

■

The Work Continues…

*After nearly two decades,
I still have some side effects
from the brain surgery.
Often, when I am not feeling well,
I do these* **Feel-Better Pathways**,
and am continually helped by them.

I hope they'll work for you, too!

Mary